LONDON

LONDON

TREASURED CAPITAL OF THE UNITED KINGDOM

ALASTAIR HORNE

amber
BOOKS

First published in 2019

Copyright © 2019 Amber Books Ltd.

Published by Amber Books Ltd
United House
North Road
London N7 9DP
United Kingdom
www.amberbooks.co.uk
Instagram: amberbooksltd
Facebook: www.facebook.com/amberbooks
Twitter: @amberbooks

Project Editor: Sarah Uttridge
Design: Trudi and Gary Webb
Picture Research: Terry Forshaw

ISBN: 978-1-78274-779-6

Printed in China

4 6 8 10 9 7 5 3 2

Contents

Introduction

Almost 20 centuries after its foundation by the Romans in around 47 AD, London remains one of the world's most famous and best-loved cities. It is a place whose history can be told through its iconic landmarks, from the Norman-era buildings of the Tower of London and Westminster Abbey to the towering skyscrapers and sporting citadels of our present century. It is a city of culture, the setting of so many of Dickens's novels, from the *Pickwick Papers* to *Great Expectations*, and the home of Shakespeare's Globe theatre, painstakingly reconstructed in Southwark almost four centuries after the original building was destroyed by fire. In this book, we'll see the city by day and by night, and watch its inhabitants travelling by train, boat, bike, bus and taxi, exploring its restaurants and markets, its bars and pubs, and its many beautiful parks and green spaces. We'll enjoy a taste of London's great diversity, perhaps best expressed in its food and drink, whose ingredients and recipes are drawn from all over the world before becoming integral parts of the city's own culture. And we'll learn why London still attracts millions of visitors each year.

ABOVE:
Flight Club, Bloomsbury
London's countless bars add glamour
and excitement to many a night out.

OPPOSITE:
Tower Bridge
One of London's most iconic landmarks.

Everyday London

Home to more than eight million people, London is so much more than just a tourist destination. At its heart lies the river Thames, which has brought both people and produce into the city for millennia, supplying the many markets which today, from Camden in the North to Brixton in the South, sell everything from crafts to cheese, and flowers to fashion. We'll follow the Thames's many transformations over the centuries, through the land reclamation that created Chelsea Embankment in the 1800s to the artificial beaches that have popped up on its banks in recent years.

London is also a city of culture. It has been a place for performance since before the time of Shakespeare's Globe, which stands today once more on the banks of the river in Southwark, painstakingly recreated from documentary evidence of the original structure. Meanwhile, West End theatres host a range of shows from Christie's *Mousetrap* at St Martin's to *Les Misérables* at the Queen's, playing to packed houses every night.

In this chapter, we'll visit the city's markets and theatres, and catch glimpses of the street performers and carnivals that help give London its unique character, from Covent Garden's buskers to the samba drummers from Brazil. We'll see the skyscrapers that are rapidly changing the city's skyline, and the Londoners who work in them, watching them live, play, worship, and shop in this busiest of cities.

OPPOSITE:
Carnaby Street
Built in the late seventeenth century, Carnaby Street has been one of London's most fashionable locations since the 1960s. Designer John Stephen, later known as the 'King of Carnaby Street', moved his 'His Clothes' shop there in 1957; Mary Quant and Foale and Tuffin soon followed suit.

OPPOSITE:
Second-hand book stalls under Waterloo Bridge
London's closest equivalent to Paris's traditional riverside 'bouquiniste' booksellers, the market on Queen's Walk is open daily on the south bank of the Thames, selling second-hand and antique books and prints in the shade of Waterloo Bridge.

ABOVE LEFT:
Brick Lane
For more than two centuries Brick Lane, in London's East End, has been a home to people arriving in Britain from abroad, including Huguenots escaping religious persecution in eighteenth century France and Ashkenazi Jews in the nineteenth century; it now lies at the heart of London's Bangladeshi community.

ABOVE RIGHT:
Railway bridge at Camden Lock
After traffic on London's once-popular Regent's Canal collapsed, the area around Camden Lock was redeveloped in the 1970s into workshops for craftspeople. Its many markets, selling clothing, food, and crafts, attract more than 100,000 visitors every weekend.

Cyclists pass mural in Hackney Wick
Cycling has become an increasingly popular mode of transport in London since the turn of the millennium, with the number of journeys by bike doubling between 2000 and 2012. The city's first dedicated cycle lane was opened in 1934 by Transport Minister Leslie Hore-Belisha.

View of the Thames from Tower Bridge
Several of the skyscrapers recently built near the Thames have been given nicknames by Londoners: here we see, from left to right, the Shard, 20 Fenchurch Street (known as the 'Walkie-Talkie'), 122 Leadenhall Street (the 'Cheesegrater'), and 30 St Mary Axe (the 'Gherkin').

Inside Covent Garden market

Markets have been held at Covent Garden since the seventeenth century, and the current market building (pictured here) was opened in 1830. Alfred Hitchcock's father worked here as a greengrocer, and the director filmed several scenes from his 1972 film *Frenzy* here.

LEFT:

**Buskers play at
Covent Garden**

Street performers have been
a popular feature at Covent
Garden since at least the
seventeenth century, when
Samuel Pepys recorded in his
diary having seen the Italian
puppeteer Signor Bologna
put on a Punch and Judy
show. Today's performers
are predominantly classical
vocalists and instrumentalists,
and variety or circus acts.

OPPOSITE:

**Batala drumming band
perform in the rain**

London's many street festivals
and carnivals celebrate
the city's diverse cultural
heritage. Here, members of
the Batala Samba–Reggae
drumming band perform
a style of percussion that
originated in the Bahia
region of Brazil.

LEFT:

Telephone boxes on Broad Street, Covent Garden

The design of London's distinctive red telephone boxes was inspired by the dome of Sir John Soane's mausoleum in Old St Pancras churchyard; designer Sir Giles Gilbert Scott had originally intended them to be painted silver, with a blue-green interior.

RIGHT:

City workers get their shoes polished near Leadenhall Market

Professional shoe-shiners can still be found around the financial districts of the City of London and in affluent areas such as Mayfair and St James's. Here, a pair of shoe-shine workers polish shoes outside Leadenhall Market.

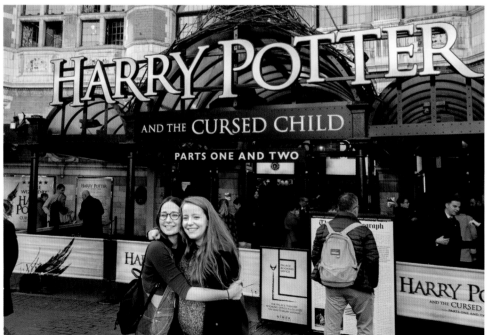

OPPOSITE TOP:

The Mousetrap at St Martin's Theatre

Agatha Christie's play *The Mousetrap* began its record-breaking run at the Ambassadors Theatre in London's West End in November 1952; it transferred to the larger St. Martin's Theatre in 1974 and has been running there ever since.

OPPOSITE BOTTOM:

Harry Potter at the Palace Theatre

The Palace Theatre was commissioned by Richard D'Oyly Carte, who intended it to become the home of English Grand Opera; since 2016, it has staged Jack Thorne's two-part play *Harry Potter and the Cursed Child.*

OPPOSITE RIGHT:

Les Misérables at the Queen's Theatre

Opening in 1907, the Queen's Theatre has, since 2004, been the home of *Les Misérables*, the adaptation of Victor Hugo's nineteenth-century French novel, which opened at the Barbican in 1985 and has since become the longest-running West End musical.

LEFT:

Pride and Prejudice at Regent's Park Open Air Theatre

Founded in 1932 by Robert Atkins and Sydney Carroll, Regent's Park Open Air Theatre runs an 18-week season every summer.

LEFT:

On stage at the Globe theatre

Built on the banks of the Thames, Shakespeare's Globe is a largely faithful reconstruction of an Elizabethan playhouse that stood nearby; its thatched roof is the only one allowed in London since the great fire of 1666.

ABOVE:

Outside the Globe

The original theatre caught fire during a production of Shakespeare's Henry VIII in 1613, when a cannon used in the performance set light to the building's wooden beams and thatched roof. The project to rebuild the theatre began in 1970 and was led by American actor, director and producer Sam Wanamaker.

Winter swimming at Hampstead Ponds
The ponds at Hampstead Heath were originally dug as reservoirs but now serve as freshwater open-air swimming pools, run by the City of London Corporation. Separate men's and women's ponds are open all year round.

RIGHT:

Blizzard on Battersea Bridge
London's roads and pavements may be rendered treacherous by winter snow and ice, but the river Thames has not frozen solid since February 1814, when it became the venue for the final five-day Frost Fair, with fairground booths, puppet shows and roundabouts.

Ice rink at Somerset House
The eighteenth-century courtyard at Somerset House, designed by Sir William Chambers in 1776, has played host to a winter ice rink for almost two decades. From 1789 to 2013, the buildings housed a range of government revenue services, including the Tax Office and most recently HM Revenue & Customs.

ABOVE:

The London Marathon

First run in 1981, the London Marathon follows a 26.2-mile route from Blackheath to the Mall. The first race saw just under 7000 runners attempt the course; by 2018, more than 41,000 runners were involved, and all but 748 completed it.

LEFT:

Marathon runners pass the *Cutty Sark*

The clipper ship *Cutty Sark*, which stands in Greenwich not far from the National Maritime Museum, takes its name from a nickname given to the witch Nannie Dee in Robert Burns's poem 'Tam o' Shanter'. Its figurehead depicts Dee holding a grey horse's tail.

ABOVE:

The prayer hall at London Central Mosque
The first purpose-built London mosque was the Fazi
Mosque in Wandsworth, built in 1926. The London Central
Mosque (pictured here) opened in Regent's Park in 1978,
and interconnects with the Islamic Culture Centre next door,
established in 1944.

RIGHT:

**The golden dome and minaret of the
London Central Mosque**
Designed by the architect Sir Frederick Gibberd, the London
Central Mosque includes two prayer halls, an entrance hall,
a large reference library and reading room, administration
areas, and a 42.5 m-tall (140-ft-tall) minaret. Its golden dome
is decorated with traditional Islamic shapes.

Brahmotsavam chariot festival

The Brahmotsavam chariot festival takes place each year, organized by the Sri Mahalakshmi Hindu Temple in East Ham. The chariot is pulled through the streets of East London to the sound of trumpets and drums.

Vaisakhi festival celebrations at City Hall

The arrival of His Highness Maharaja Sir Duleep Singh in London in 1854 first brought Sikhism to Britain. Today, the city is home to the Gurdwara Sri Guru Singh Sabha, the largest Sikh temple outside India, which opened in 2003 in Southall in the London borough of Ealing.

Apartment buildings at St George Wharf
Work on St George Wharf in Vauxhall was completed in 2012; the riverside development includes more than 1000 apartments, plus offices, restaurants and retail units. The St George Wharf Tower is the tallest residential building in Britain.

OPPOSITE:
Houses on Chelsea Embankment
Opened in 1874 by the Duke of Edinburgh, Chelsea Embankment reclaimed more than 21 hectares (52 acres) of land from the Thames and covered key parts of the city's new sewerage system. Designed by civil engineer Sir Joseph Bazalgette, it cost more than £270,000 (£2.8 million in today's money) to build.

Piccadilly Circus

One of London's best-known and busiest junctions, Piccadilly Circus connects Regent Street, Shaftesbury Avenue, Coventry Street, Waterloo Place, and Piccadilly itself. Its famous central statue is not actually of Eros, as most people believe, but of his brother Anteros, the Greek God of requited love.

LEFT:
The Savoy Hotel
London's first luxury hotel, The Savoy opened in 1889, owned by a consortium led by theatrical impresario Richard D'Oyly Carte, whose Savoy Theatre stands next door. George Gershwin's *Rhapsody in Blue* received its first UK performance here in 1925, broadcast by the BBC from the hotel.

OPPOSITE:
City workers eat their lunch beside the Paternoster sculpture
Elisabeth Frink's sculpture of a shepherd and his sheep can be found in Paternoster Square, between St Paul's Cathedral and the London Stock Exchange. Nearby Paternoster Row was formerly the site of Newgate Market, one of London's largest wholesale meat markets.

LEFT:
St George's Day in Leadenhall Market
Dating back to the early fourteenth century, Leadenhall Market stands at the heart of the City of London. The present building was designed in 1881 by the architect Sir Horace Jones, then redecorated in the 1990s.

TOP RIGHT:
Columbia Road Flower Market
The colourful Columbia Road Flower Market originally opened on Saturdays, before an act of parliament was passed allowing trading on a Sunday, to benefit the many Jewish merchants who were unable to work on their Sabbath. It now opens every Sunday from 8 a.m. to 2 p.m.

BOTTOM RIGHT:
Tights and stockings at Brixton's markets
Brixton's many markets and covered arcades are justly famous. Electric Avenue, built in the 1880s, was the first market street to be lit by electricity, and gave its name to reggae singer Eddy Grant's 1982 single, which reached number two on both sides of the Atlantic.

ABOVE:
Enjoying the beach on the banks of the Thames
Though London lies many miles from Britain's coast, many
artificial beaches pop up in the city every summer, from the
Urban London Beach at the Royal Docks to the Southbank
Centre Beach, a giant sandpit on the banks of the Thames.

RIGHT:
Children play in Jeppe Hein's water sculpture
Jeppe Hein's water sculpture Appearing Rooms has been
a regular summer feature outside the Southbank Centre's
Queen Elizabeth Hall for more than a decade. Its watery walls
rise and fall randomly, creating new structures each time,
combining a meditation on space with an opportunity to cool
off on a hot day.

Sun breaks through the clouds over London
Flowing through the heart of London, the Thames is crossed by 33 bridges within the city limits. The newest of these is the Millennium Bridge, seen here between Southwark and Blackfriars bridges; opening in June 2000, it then closed the same day after starting to sway alarmingly, and did not reopen until 2002.

Food and Drink

Whatever your tastes, you'll find something to delight your appetite in London. From Brick Lane to Brixton, Canary Wharf to Spitalfields, its historic markets and fashionable restaurants offer a wide range of food from all around the world, whether you're looking for Lincolnshire potatoes and Yorkshire rhubarb, truffles from Australia, or Caribbean barbecued chicken.

If it's a drink that you're after, then there'll be something to quench your thirst in one of the city's traditional pubs or stylish bars and cafes, whether you prefer a pint of bitter at the Churchill Arms, a glass of dry white wine from Britain's oldest wine and spirits merchant, one of the myriad teas available at Harrods, or a glass of champagne at Claridge's.

Here, too, you'll find the meals that have come to define the British menu: a full English breakfast, with its bacon, eggs, beans and sausages; an afternoon tea of cakes and buttered scones in a fancy hotel dining room; fish and chips – introduced from Eastern Europe; or pie and mash with jellied eels.

Prepare yourself also for a taste of the unexpected. In this chapter, you'll find riverside igloos for al fresco dining in all weathers, a pub bedecked with almost a hundred Christmas trees, and frozen yoghurt served from a bus; you can even take a drink with Sherlock Holmes and his companion Dr Watson, or eat alongside art by Banksy. Is your mouth watering already?

OPPOSITE:
Shrimp curry in Borough Market
One of London's oldest food markets, Southwark's Borough Market is said to have been in existence for more than a millennium on various sites in the area. In recent years, it has combined selling wholesale fruit and vegetables to greengrocers with offering artisanal foods like this shrimp curry – to the public.

RIGHT:

Borough Market entrance
The buildings currently housing the market were designed by Henry Rose in 1851 and have been added to since then; the market gained its Southwark Street art deco entrance in 1932, and in 2004 the South Portico, originally part of the Floral Hall at Covent Garden, was re-erected here as part of a major site refurbishment.

OPPOSITE TOP RIGHT:

Morning at the market
Since 1906, the market has been owned by a charitable trust, and is now run by a board of volunteer trustees. It opens six days a week – Monday to Saturday – and on Sundays in December.

OPPOSITE BOTTOM RIGHT:

Colourful fruit stall
Borough Market sells fruit and vegetables from across Britain and beyond: organic fruit from Kent, tomatoes from the Isle of Wight, Lincolnshire potatoes, Yorkshire rhubarb and even truffles from Australia.

RIGHT:

Fresh fish at Brixton Market
Brixton has long been known for its fishmongers, selling everything from seabass to salmon, and haddock to hake. Though some historic traders have been driven out of the area in recent years by rising rents and redevelopment, many remain.

ABOVE:

Fruit and veg at Walthamstow Market

Stretching for around a kilometre (two-thirds of a mile), from one end of the high street almost to the other, Walthamstow Market is Europe's longest outdoor market. Its 500 or so stalls, selling fabric, clothes, bags, and a wide range of food, are open five days a week, from Tuesday to Saturday.

RIGHT:

Fresh tomatoes on the vine

The market first opened in 1885, as the development of the railways transformed Walthamstow from a rural village into a busy London suburb; its population doubled every ten years between 1871 and 1901.

TOP LEFT:
All the trimmings at Brick Lane Market
There are many street food stalls to be found around Brick Lane's busy market, selling everything from burgers to buffalo wings. Ely's Yard, behind the Truman Brewery on the west side of the lane, hosts foods from all over the world alongside work by street artist Banksy.

OPPOSITE:
Sizzling barbecued chicken at Notting Hill Carnival
Taking place each year during the August Bank Holiday weekend, the Notting Hill Carnival is one of the world's largest street festivals. More than 200 food stalls line the route, offering a wide range of Caribbean street food, including this barbecued chicken.

BOTTOM LEFT:
Colourful Moroccan food
The nearby Boiler House, at 152 Brick Lane, is one of London's newest food halls. With more than 30 stands, it offers a truly international culinary experience, with food from countries including Morocco, Poland, Ethiopia, Korea and Malaysia.

OPPOSITE:
African food at Spitalfields Market
There has been a market at Spitalfields since the seventeenth century; since 2013, an annual African Market run by Pop Up Africa has taken place on the Spring Bank Holiday, with around 100 stalls selling food from countries including Ghana, Ethiopia and Nigeria.

RIGHT:
A full English breakfast
A traditional full English breakfast – also known as a 'fry-up' – usually consists of bacon, eggs, sausages, tomatoes, mushrooms, beans and toast. Vegetarian versions often substitute the sausages and bacon for hash browns and vegetarian sausages.

ABOVE:

Igloos at the Coppa Club

Open from October until January, these Perspex capsules at the Coppa Club's riverside restaurant offer one of London's more unusual eating experiences: al fresco winter dining in the warm, with views across the Thames to the Shard and Tower Bridge.

OPPOSITE:

Waterfront restaurant, Canary Wharf

The past 30 years have seen the wholesale redevelopment of Canary Wharf into one of London's main financial centres, following the closure of its docks in the 1980s. Its many restaurants and bars cater to the varied tastes of city workers.

Pie and mash and mushy peas

A traditional working-class meal, pie and mash became popular in London's East End during Victorian times. It was often accompanied by jellied eels fished from the Thames and cooked in gelatine. Pie and mash shops began to appear in London in the mid-nineteenth century, and a few remain open today.

The Great British Fish and Chip Shop

Celebrating one of Britain's favourite meals, The Great British Fish and Chip Shop stood on King William Walk in Greenwich until 2012, when it was replaced by Goddards at Greenwich, selling another British staple: pie and mash.

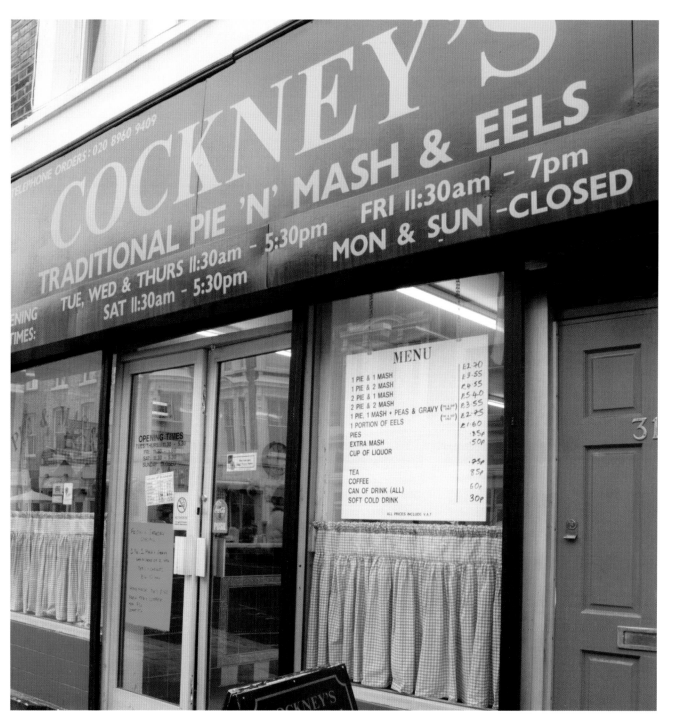

ABOVE:

Pints on the bar in a London pub

London's 3500 pubs are often the focal points of their communities, but their numbers are declining: 1300 have shut down since the turn of the millennium, with one pub closing every week, on average.

RIGHT:

The Albert on Victoria Street

The Albert first opened in the 1860s, built on the site of an earlier pub, The Blue Coat Boy. Named, like so many British pubs, after Queen Victoria's husband Prince Albert, its picturesque frontage, seen here, survived the Blitz and is now protected by law.

**The Churchill Arms
at Christmas**
Its colourful flower displays,
which cost an estimated
£25,000 each year, have won
prizes at the Chelsea Flower
Show, but The Churchill Arms
excels itself each Christmas:
a record 90 trees and 21,000
lights adorned the building
in 2016.

The Sherlock Holmes, Northumberland Street
Not far from Charing Cross Station, the Sherlock Holmes pub began life as a small hotel, under which guises it features in the Conan Doyle story *The Adventure of the Noble Bachelor*. Today it is not only a pub but also home to a recreation of Holmes and Watson's study and sitting room, originally created for the Festival of Britain in 1951.

Frozen yoghurt sold from a bus on London's Southbank
Some of London's older buses have been repurposed to offer unconventional dining experiences. The Crust Conductor serves pizzas at Peckham Rye during the winter and travels the festival circuit in the summer, while this pink-painted Routemaster bus sold yoghurt on the Southbank in 2014.

ABOVE:

Tea at the Connaught hotel
Opened in 1815 as the Prince of Saxe-Coburg Hotel, the Connaught hotel adopted its current name in 1917, during World War I. Also changing its name from Saxe-Coburg that year was the British royal family, which became the house of Windsor.

OPPOSITE:

Specialty teas at Harrods Food Hall
Harrods, in Knightsbridge, is one of the world's best-known department stores. Its founder, Charles Henry Harrod, was a grocer and tea trader, and the store now has its own 'tea tailor', creating personalized blends of teas for customers.

RIGHT:

Claridge's afternoon tea
Afternoon tea at Claridge's five-star hotel is a sumptuous experience. Anna Maria, the seventh Duchess of Bedford, is thought to have been the inventor of what became an ubiquitous social ritual for wealthier Victorians. Today, sandwiches, scones and cakes are often accompanied by cocktails or even champagne.

**Gordon Ramsey's
Maze restaurant**
Gordon Ramsey's restaurant
Maze opened in Mayfair in
2005, combining European
and Asian influences, with
its sushi bar, Asian fusion
cocktail menu and selection
of small plate dishes.

ABOVE:

Wine merchants Berry Bros. & Rudd
Trading since 1698 from its premises in London's St James's Street, Berry Bros. & Rudd is Britain's oldest wine and spirits merchant, now with offices in Hong Kong, Japan and Singapore. Founded by the Widow Bourne as a grocer's, it originally sold coffee to the area's coffee houses, before focusing on wines and spirits.

Landmarks

London is a city of landmarks, whose rich history can be traced through its buildings and monuments. From the Norman period still stand the eleventh-century Tower of London, established following the conquest in 1066, and Westminster Abbey, built between 1245 and 1269 to replace an earlier church on the site. St Paul's Cathedral and the Royal Observatory at Greenwich both date from Stuart times, while the Victorian period is particularly prominent with its museums at Kensington and Bloomsbury, the Palace of Westminster, its 'magnificent seven' cemeteries, and Trafalgar Square.

The past few decades have left as large a mark on the city as any before. New landmarks have arisen. Some, like the London Eye and the O2, were originally part of the city's Millennium celebrations, while others, such as the London Aquatics Centre and the Lee Valley VeloPark, form part of the legacy of the 2012 Olympics. Some of the city's most historic sporting venues have been either improved – like Wimbledon – or rebuilt entirely, like Wembley Stadium. The city's skyline has also been transformed by the arrival of several waves of skyscrapers, from One Canada Square in the 1990s to the Gherkin and the Shard in the past decade. Recent years have also seen the renewal and repurposing of historic landmarks: Bankside Power Station became the Tate Modern gallery, and a new telescope was installed at the Royal Observatory.

London, however, retains its historic character: its Norman, Stuart and Victorian inheritance stands alongside these new developments, just as St Paul's Cathedral stands beneath the shadow of the Shard.

OPPOSITE:
The Royal Albert Hall
Opened by Queen Victoria and her son the Prince of Wales in 1871, the Royal Albert Hall has hosted the Proms – an eight-week season of classical concerts founded by Sir Henry Wood – each year since 1941. Early performances were marred by a pronounced echo; today, 85 acoustic diffusers, nicknamed 'mushrooms', hang from the auditorium's ceiling to stop sound reverberating from there.

Zebra crossing, Abbey Road
Made famous by its appearance on the cover of the Beatles' 1969 album *Abbey Road*, which shows the band's four members crossing the road near their recording studio, the zebra crossing at Abbey Road is regularly visited by fans attempting their own recreations of that cover; it now has grade II listed status, protecting it from redevelopment.

The Royal Observatory at Greenwich
Commissioned by King Charles II and designed by Sir Christopher Wren, the Royal Observatory at Greenwich opened in 1676. During the twentieth century, the building lost most of its scientific functions and became a museum, but in 2018, a new telescope, the Annie Maunder Astrographic Telescope, was installed at the site.

Battersea Power Station
The iconic Battersea Power Station is perhaps best known outside London for its appearance on the cover of Pink Floyd's 1977 album *Animal*s. It comprised two separate stations within a single structure: station A was built in the 1930s and closed in 1975; station B, opened in the 1950s and closed eight years later in 1983.

LEFT:

The tomb of Karl Marx at Highgate Cemetery

Though Marx was originally buried elsewhere in Highgate's Eastern Cemetery, his remains – and those of his wife and other family members – were moved in 1954 to their present location, where this monument was unveiled two years later. Occasionally vandalized, and twice attacked with bombs during the 1970s, it is now a listed structure.

OPPOSITE:

Circle of Lebanon, Highgate Cemetery

Opened in 1839, Highgate Cemetery was the third of London's 'magnificent seven' Victorian cemeteries to be built in the decade between 1832 and 1841 to overcome overcrowding in the city's parish graveyards. This picture shows the inner part of the West Cemetery's Circle of Lebanon; Victorian lesbian novelist Marguerite Radclyffe Hall is buried here.

Canary Wharf at sunset
Built on the site of the West India Docks, which closed in 1980 after more than 175 years, Canary Wharf extends over almost 40 hectares (100 acres) and houses many of the tallest buildings in Europe, including One Canada Square, with its distinctive pyramid roof.

OVERLEAF LEFT:
Inside the British Museum
Opened in 1759 to house a collection of more than 70,000 objects bequeathed to the nation by the collector Sir Hans Sloane, the British Museum now receives six million visitors each year. From 1857 until 1997, its circular Reading Room (pictured) housed the collection of books now held by the British Library.

PREVIOUS PAGES RIGHT:
30 St Mary Axe, also known as the 'Gherkin'
Built on the former site of the Baltic Exchange and the Chamber of Shipping, 30 St Mary Axe was designed by Sir Norman Foster and houses offices plus a restaurant and bar.

PREVIOUS PAGES FAR RIGHT:
The Lloyds Building, Lime Street
The Lloyd's Building was designed by architect Lord Richard Rogers and opened in 1986. As with Paris's Pompidou Centre, co-designed by Rogers, its services – such as lifts and ducting – are found on the outside of the building, maximizing the space inside.

LEFT:
The Shard
More than 300m (1000 feet) high, the Shard is the United Kingdom's tallest building. Its top 23 floors comprise its spire, with the next four floors, from 69 to 72, occupied by viewing platforms open to the public.

LEFT:

The O2 Arena, Greenwich
Built beneath the Millennium Dome, part of London's celebrations for the year 2000, the O2 Arena has hosted concerts by artists such as Prince, Bon Jovi and the Rolling Stones, and sporting events such as the 2012 Olympics and, since 2009, tennis's ATP World Tour Finals.

The Thames Barrier
Stretching 500m (1600 feet) across the river near Woolwich, the Thames Barrier comprises ten steel gates that can be raised to form a barrier five storeys high against flooding. It has been put into use more than 180 times since it first came into operation in 1982.

LEFT:

St Paul's Cathedral from the Millennium Bridge
Designed by Sir Christopher Wren to replace a Norman cathedral destroyed by the great fire of London, work began on the new St Paul's Cathedral in 1675; the final stone of the main structure was laid in 1708. Despite being struck twice by bombs during the Blitz in World War II, the cathedral survived with only minor damage.

Inside the cathedral
St Paul's Cathedral remains
an active site of worship,
hosting at least four services
daily. Its grand organ, built
in 1695, has more than 7000
pipes and five keyboards;
buried in its crypt are Lord
Nelson and Lord Wellington.

Leadenhall Market
The ornate wrought iron and glass structure of Leadenhall Market has featured in many films, including *Harry Potter and the Philosopher's Stone* and *The Imaginarium of Dr Parnassus*. The course of the 2012 Olympic Marathon also passed through the market.

Admiralty Arch

Commissioned in memory of Queen Victoria by her son, King Edward VII, Admiralty Arch was funded by public donations. It originally housed government offices but in 2012, on the hundredth anniversary of its completion, it was sold to developers for conversion into a hotel, restaurants and apartments.

Changing of the guard at Buckingham Palace
One of the most popular ceremonies for visitors to London,
the Changing of the Guard takes place outside Buckingham
Palace at 11 a.m. every Monday, Wednesday, Friday and Sunday.
Dressed in their famous red tunics and bearskin hats, members
of the Queen's Guard exchange the royal standard with their
replacements.

Buckingham Palace and Queen Victoria Memorial
Buckingham Palace became the main royal residence in 1837
when Queen Victoria acceded to the throne upon the death of
her uncle King William IV. Built for the Duke of Buckingham
in 1703 and expanded many times since then, it comprises 775
rooms, including 78 bathrooms.

LEFT:

A Yeoman Warder, or 'beefeater', walks among ceramic poppies

To commemorate the centenary of the outbreak of World War I in 2014, the moat at the Tower of London was filled with 888,246 ceramic poppies, each one representing a British or Colonial serviceman killed during the war. The installation, entitled *Blood Swept Lands and Seas of Red*, was created by Tom Piper and Paul Cummins.

OPPOSITE:

The Tower of London by night

The Tower of London served as a prison from 1100 until the mid-twentieth century; its first prisoner, Ranulf Flambard, the Bishop of Durham, escaped in 1101 using a rope that had been smuggled to him in a gallon of wine. Later prisoners included Princess Elizabeth – the future Queen Elizabeth I, Anne Boleyn, Guy Fawkes, and Rudolf Hess.

LEFT:

10 Downing Street

The official residence of the British Prime Minister, 10 Downing Street has been a government building since 1732 and contains around 100 rooms. Its famous black door cannot be opened from the outside, and therefore the building can never be left empty.

OPPOSITE:

Choirboys at Westminster Abbey

Since William the Conqueror in 1066, every monarch of England – and, latterly, Britain – has been crowned at Westminster Abbey. The present church was built between 1245 and 1269, under the orders of King Henry III.

The Palace of Westminster
Home to both Houses of
Parliament, the present
Palace of Westminster was
built between 1840 and 1852
after the previous building
was almost completely
destroyed by fire in 1834.
It had previously escaped
destruction in 1605 when
the Gunpowder Plot led
by Robert Catesby was
discovered before it could
be carried out.

View of the Palace of Westminster from the London Eye

Opened in 2000, the giant Ferris wheel known as the London Eye stands on the south bank of the river Thames, its 32 oval capsules offering views across the city. It was originally intended as a temporary attraction but was made permanent in 2002.

OPPOSITE:

The London Eye from across the river Thames

The London Eye's 120m (400ft) diameter wheel rotates fully once every half hour, travelling at a speed of 26cm (10 inches) per second, slowly enough that most of its 3.75 million annual passengers can alight and disembark without it stopping.

LEFT:

Nelson's Column in Trafalgar Square

Trafalgar Square opened in 1844 to commemorate Britain's naval victory at the Battle of Trafalgar in October 1805. At its centre stands Nelson's Column, 52m (169 ft) high, built between 1840 and 1843.

RIGHT:

Aerial view of Trafalgar Square

The fourth plinth at Trafalgar Square remained empty until 1999, after insufficient funding was obtained for the planned statue of William IV. Since then, it has mostly housed a series of temporary sculptures, including David Shrigley's 'Really Good', a comic bronze cast of a hand giving a thumbs-up sign, and Katharina Fritsch's blue cockerel.

Bankside Power Station, now home to Tate Modern
Built in 1891 to supply electricity to Southwark and the City of London, Bankside Power Station was decommissioned in 1981 and stood empty for almost two decades before reopening in 2000 as the home of the Tate Modern museum and art gallery.

OPPOSITE:

Inside the National Gallery
Founded in 1824 when the British government bought a collection of 38 paintings from the heirs of John Julius Angerstein, the National Gallery now houses more than 2300 works of art. It moved to its present site at Trafalgar Square in 1838.

LEFT:

The central hall of the Natural History Museum
The Natural History Museum opened in 1881 to house the British Museum's growing collection of natural history items. A replica diplodocus skeleton stood in the central hall from the 1970s until 2017, when it was replaced by a blue whale skeleton.

OPPOSITE:

The front entrance to the Natural History Museum
Designed by architect Alfred Waterhouse, the Natural History Museum has been described as a 'cathedral to nature'. Waterhouse used terracotta tiles to protect the building from London pollution.

NATURAL HISTORY MUSEUM

LEFT:

Medieval and Renaissance Galleries at the Victoria and Albert Museum
The Victoria and Albert Museum adopted its present name in 1899 at one of Queen Victoria's final public engagements: the laying of the foundation stone for the Aston Webb building.

OPPOSITE:

The Victoria and Albert Museum
Intended by its first director Henry Cole to serve as a 'schoolroom for everyone', the Victoria and Albert Museum was opened in 1857, as the South Kensington Museum, by Queen Victoria. It houses more than 2.3 million objects from the history of art and design.

LEFT:

No. 1 Court, Wimbledon
The All England Lawn
Tennis and Croquet Club
has hosted the Wimbledon
Championships, the world's
oldest tennis tournament,
for two weeks every summer
since 1877, except during
wartime. Here we see the new
No. 1 Court, opened in 1997.

PREVIOUS PAGES:

**Old Royal Naval College,
Greenwich**
The Royal Naval College was
established in 1873 when the
Naval College in Portsmouth
took over the buildings
formerly belonging to
Greenwich's Royal Hospital
for Seamen. In 1998, the
college opened to the public
as a heritage site.

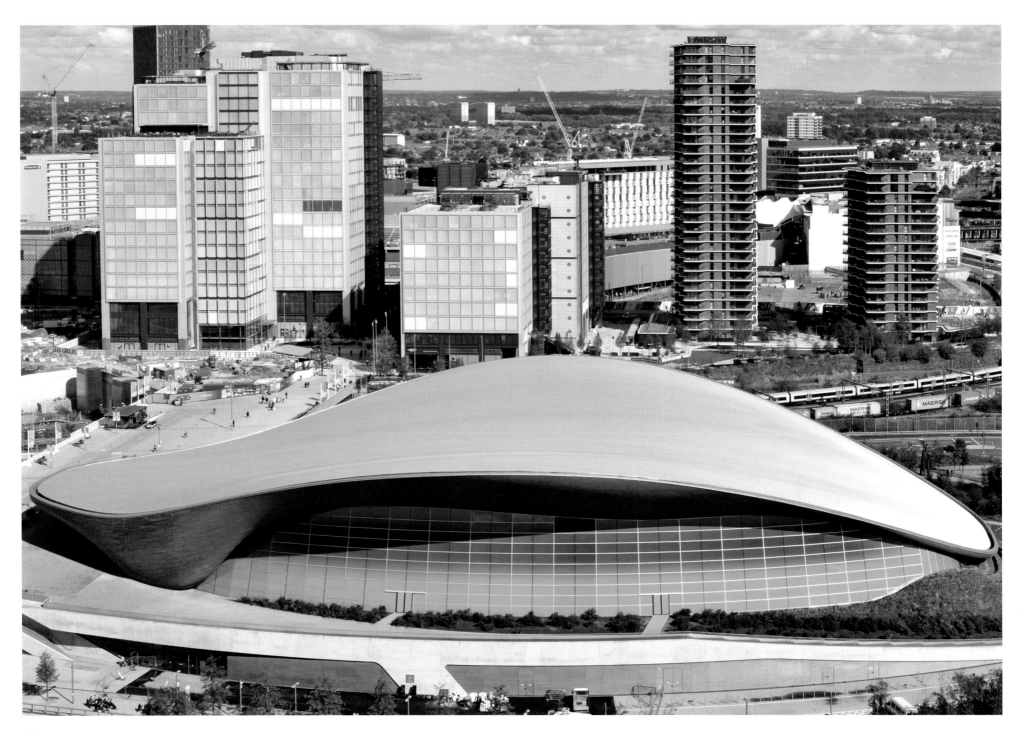

OPPOSITE:

**The London Aquatics Centre at the Queen Elizabeth
Olympic Park**

Designed by Zaha Hadid and built for the 2012 Olympics, the
London Aquatics Centre opened to the public in 2014. Its two
Olympic-sized swimming pools have moveable floors to change
the depth of the water.

ABOVE:

Wembley Stadium

The current Wembley Stadium opened in 2007, replacing the
original stadium that stood on the site between 1923 and 2003.
Its most striking feature is the 315m (1030 ft) long arch,
133 m (440 ft) tall at its highest point, which supports the
entire weight of the north roof.

Parks and Green Spaces

Despite its reputation as a bustling metropolis, man-made and urban from the tips of the skyscrapers that dominate its skyline all the way down to the deepest of its underground tunnels, London is also a surprisingly green city. Its eight Royal Parks stretch across 2000 hectares (5000 acres), from Richmond Park and Bushy Park in the south-west to Regent's Park in the north, providing plentiful spaces for rest and relaxation.

In addition to these historic parks can be found more than 3000 other green spaces, from the small garden squares seen in many of London's more stylish areas – such as Russell Square and Soho Square – to the huge expanses of Hampstead Heath and Epping Forest. Such places provide habitats for a rich diversity of flora and fauna, from the koi carp in Holland Park's Kyoto Garden to the red deer found in Richmond Park. Many too are home to sporting activities: Hyde Park has its Christmas morning swim across the Serpentine lake, while Crystal Palace Park has hosted everything from cricket matches to Formula One racing.

The city's open spaces have also proved irresistible to the city's writers, with Virginia Woolf and Dodie Smith featuring Regent's Park in their novels, Hampstead Heath appearing in both *Dracula* and John le Carré's *Smiley's People*, and J. M. Barrie even secretly placing a statue of his best-known creation, Peter Pan, in Kensington Gardens, to be discovered joyfully by children playing there.

OPPOSITE:

Tree tunnel at Crystal Palace Park
Crystal Palace Park was built between 1852 and 1854 to house the cast-iron and plate-glass building used during the 1851 Great Exhibition, which burned to the ground in 1936. It has also hosted many sporting events, including 20 FA Cup finals, almost 50 first-class cricket matches, and even speedway and Formula One racing.

Epping Forest pond
Epping Forest is London's
largest open space, stretching
across 2400 hectares (5900
acres). Home to 50,000
ancient pollard trees and more
than 100 ponds and lakes, it
has been designated a Site of
Special Scientific Interest.

Epping Forest in autumn
Laws were introduced in the twelfth century protecting the rights of common people to graze pigs and cattle in the forest, and to gather wood, while preventing all but the king from hunting there. Around 50 cows are still grazed there today.

Red deer in Richmond Park
London's largest Royal Park, Richmond Park became a hunting ground for red and fallow deer when King Charles I moved his court to nearby Richmond Palace to escape the plague in 1625. Today, more than 630 deer roam freely through the park.

Kyoto Garden at Holland Park

Holland Park once formed the grounds of Holland House, a Jacobean country house destroyed by bombing during the Blitz. The park's Kyoto Garden is a traditional Japanese garden including stone lanterns, Japanese maple trees, and a pond full of Koi carp

LEFT:

Colourful trees at the Kyoto Garden, Holland Park

Opened in 1991, the Kyoto Garden was a gift from the city of Kyoto to the people of Great Britain. In 2012, a second Japanese garden was opened at the park to commemorate the Japanese people's gratitude for British support following the Fukushima disaster.

The London skyline from Parliament Hill

Part of north-west London's Hampstead Heath, Parliament Hill offers excellent views over the city's skyline. Its name is thought to derive from its use during the English Civil War by troops fighting for parliament against the king.

Hampstead Heath in winter
One of London's highest points, Hampstead Heath offers excellent opportunities for sledging during winter. It also features in many novels, including Wilkie Collins's *The Woman in White*, Bram Stoker's *Dracula*, and John le Carré's *Smiley's People*.

OVERLEAF:
Shooter's Hill in the snow
Taking its name either from its use by archers as a practice ground, or from its popularity with highwaymen and footpads, Shooter's Hill is one of London's highest points, with views of the Thames and central London.

125

Squirrel in Hyde Park

London's largest Royal Park, Hyde Park was taken by King Henry VIII in 1536 from the monks of Westminster Abbey and established as a private park for hunting deer. A century later, King Charles I opened it to the public.

Hyde Park deckchairs

Though Hyde Park is now a popular spot for relaxation, it has had a somewhat bloody history. Many duels were fought in the park in the eighteenth century, and military executions also took place here.

Aerial view of the Serpentine, Hyde Park
Created in 1730 on the orders of Queen Caroline, wife of King George II, the Serpentine is a popular location for swimming and boating. Since 1864, it has hosted the Peter Pan swimming race every Christmas morning and during the 2012 London Olympics, it was the venue for the triathlon and marathon swimming events.

ABOVE:

Plaque from Diana Memorial Walk, Kensington Gardens

Marked by 90 plaques set in the ground, the Diana Princess of Wales Memorial Walk passes through four Royal Parks on its seven-mile trail through London locations associated with the princess.

LEFT:

Diana memorial garden, Kensington Palace

In 2017, the sunken garden at Kensington Palace, on the western edge of Hyde Park, was transformed into the Diana memorial garden, to honour the princess who lived in the palace until her death in 1997.

OPPOSITE:

Diana Memorial Fountain, Hyde Park

Opened by Her Majesty the Queen in July 2004, the Memorial Fountain to Diana, Princess of Wales consists of an oval stream bed built from 545 pieces of Cornish granite.

OPPOSITE:

The Serpentine Bridge from below
Built in the 1820s by the engineer John Rennie, the Serpentine Bridge marks part of the boundary between Hyde Park and Kensington Gardens; it also divides the lake into The Long Water to the west, and the Serpentine to the east.

RIGHT:

Peter Pan statue, Kensington Gardens
The bronze statue of Peter Pan which stands to the west of The Long Water was commissioned by the author J. M. Barrie and installed in Kensington Gardens secretly – so that it might seem to have appeared magically – in 1912, without permission from the authorities.

**The Palm House,
Kew Gardens**
Designed by Decimus Burton
to recreate a rainforest
climate, the Palm House at
Kew Gardens was built by
Richard Turner and houses,
as its centrepiece, a huge
Jurassic cycad believed to
be the oldest pot plant in
the world.

**The Great Pagoda,
Kew Gardens**
Completed in 1762, Kew
Gardens' Great Pagoda
stands almost 50m (160 ft)
high, offering excellent
views to anyone willing to
climb its 253 steps. During
World War II, holes were
cut in the floors of the
building to test the flight
of British bombs.

LEFT:

Birds perch on wooden posts in Regent's Park

Designed by architect John Nash around 1811, Regent's Park was intended to house a summer palace for the Prince Regent (later King George IV), but this was never built.

OPPOSITE:

The Triton Fountain, Regent's Park

Opposite the Jubilee Gates at the heart of Regent's Park stands the Triton Fountain, at the centre of a round pool. Its sculptures of a sea god and two mermaids were designed by William McMillan.

BELOW:

Lake and footpath, Regent's Park

Regent's Park has featured in several novels, including Dodie Smith's *The Hundred and One Dalmatians*, Elizabeth Bowen's *The Heat of the Day*, and Virginia Woolf's *Mrs Dalloway*.

OVERLEAF:

View of Greenwich Park and the Old Royal Naval College

The hill at Greenwich Park offers spectacular views of London, from the National Maritime Museum, the Old Royal Naval College, and the park itself – all seen here in the foreground – to the skyscrapers of Canary Wharf in the distance.

St James's Park at sunset
London's oldest Royal Park, St James's Park took its name from a hospital for female lepers which occupied the site in the thirteenth century. King Henry VIII created a deer park in the area, then King James I landscaped the park and kept a collection of animals here, including an elephant, crocodiles and camels.

Walthamstow Wetlands nature reserve
The ten reservoirs in Walthamstow were constructed by the East London Waterworks Company between 1863 and 1904. The Walthamstow Wetlands nature reserve opened on the site in 2017, and is home to populations of diving ducks, shovelers, grey herons and little egrets.

Clapham Common at sunset
One of London's largest open spaces, Clapham Common is mentioned in the Domesday Book of 1086, and contains three ponds: Eagle Pond, Mount Pond, and the modern paddling pool Cock Pond.

OPPOSITE:

Green Park at sunrise
Established by King Charles II to provide a link between Hyde Park to the west and St James's Park to the east, Green Park was originally known as Upper St James's Park, before assuming its present name in 1746. Since 2002, it has been the site of a memorial to five million servicemen from India, Africa and the Caribbean who fought in two world wars.

UNDERGROUND
PUBLIC SUBWAY
the Coca-Cola christmas trucks are coming
TDK
New Generation
SAMSUNG

Nightlife

By day a busy workplace, by night London reveals a different, more relaxed side to its character. From the stylish new Sky Pod Bar on the 35th floor of the 'Walkie-Talkie' building to the historic inns that can trace their history back five centuries, the city's thousands of pubs, clubs, bars and restaurants offer a range of ways to unwind. The shops in the city's West End open late most nights, and more than a hundred theatres stage plays and shows each evening, while many of London's museums have special evening events once a month. And with most of the Underground network now open all through the night at weekends, it's even easier to stay out late.

Even the long, cold nights of winter are no reason to stay at home, as the Christmas lights make London shine brighter than ever; Leicester Square is transformed each year into a festive fairground, while seasonal street markets appear across the city, most famously at Southbank and at Hyde Park's Winter Wonderland. Tickets for the Midnight Mass at Westminster Abbey on Christmas Eve each year are fully-booked several weeks in advance, while the banks of the Thames and nearby open spaces are full to bursting on New Year's Eve, whatever the weather, to watch the firework display marking the end of one year and the beginning of the next.

OPPOSITE:
Underground sign at Piccadilly Circus
Transport for London launched a weekend night service on the London Underground in late 2016. Trains now run through the night on Fridays and Saturdays across the entire length of the Victoria and Jubilee lines, and partly on the Central, Northern and Piccadilly lines.

Late night shopping on Oxford Street

Oxford Street is Europe's busiest retail street, attracting more than half a million visitors every day. Many of its stores open until 9 pm during the week, and until 10 pm on Thursdays.

Drinking at a London pub

Many London pubs have fascinating histories. The Lamb and Flag in Covent Garden used to host bare-knuckle boxing matches, while the Spaniards Inn has stood on Hampstead Heath since 1585 and is said to have been visited by both Keats and Dickens.

RIGHT:

Southbank Winter Market
Part of the Southbank Centre's Winter Festival, the Winter Market is open from early November until just after Christmas, and features traders from around the world offering seasonal delights including mulled wine and handmade Christmas gifts.

OVERLEAF:

Aerial view of the Southbank and Waterloo Station
There's plenty to do after dark at the Southbank. Anyone looking for drama can visit the National Theatre, whose three auditoria stage contemporary and classic plays, and musicals; the nearby Old and Young Vic theatres; or one of the British Film Institute's four cinemas.

148

LEFT:
Christmas lights
From November until early January, many London streets are lit up by festive Christmas lights. Some of the most famous displays are to be found on Oxford Street, Carnaby Street and Bond Street, though Marylebone High Street and St Christopher's Place are also worth visiting.

ABOVE:
Busking under lights at Piccadilly Circus
The first illuminated sign at Piccadilly Circus appeared in 1908; it used incandescent light bulbs and advertised Perrier. Neon soon took over, but since the millennium, the famous signs – advertising brands including Coca-Cola, Hyundai, and McDonald's – have used LED displays.

PREVIOUS PAGES LEFT:
**Snow falling on the
Southbank and the
London Eye**
The Southbank offers
excellent views of the annual
firework display each New
Year's Eve, though tickets sell
out rapidly. The London Eye
forms the focal point of the
colourful show, which begins
after the chimes of Big Ben
ring in the New Year.

PREVIOUS PAGES RIGHT:
Westminster Abbey at night
Westminster Abbey has
hosted 16 royal weddings,
mostly recently that of Prince
William and Catherine
Middleton in 2011. Its
Midnight Mass service every
Christmas Eve is so popular
that tickets are fully booked
weeks beforehand.

RIGHT:
**Southbank Centre
Christmas Market**
London's Christmas markets
have become increasingly
popular in recent years. In
addition to market stalls,
the Southbank Centre's
Winter Festival now features
a spectacular recreation
of a historical circus,
with acrobats, jugglers,
contortionists, and life-sized
puppet elephants.

Christmas in Leicester Square
Since 2016, Leicester Square has been transformed into a winter wonderland from November until January each year. Traditional market stalls sell festive food and drink, while an authentic 1920s travelling tent hosts a range of shows; children can also visit Santa in his grotto.

New Year fireworks over Tower Bridge
More than 100,000 people watch the New Year's Eve firework display in London each year from sites along the Thames; the illuminated Tower Bridge provides a spectacular backdrop for those watching from the nearby Potters Fields Park.

LEFT:

The Comedy Store, Soho
Many of the alternative
comedians who became
popular in the 1980s first
made their names at The
Comedy Store, which opened
in Soho in 1979. Rik Mayall,
Adrian Edmondson and Nigel
Planer from the Young Ones;
the double act French and
Saunders; and Blackadder
co-writer Ben Elton all
performed there.

OPPOSITE:

The Windmill Theatre, Soho
In recent years, Soho has lost
much of its reputation for
risqué entertainment, moving
markedly upmarket. From
the 1930s to the 1960s,
though, The Windmill theatre
was a major contributor
to that reputation,
circumventing the Lord
Chamberlain's strict rules on
stage nudity by presenting
its naked performers as
unmoving statues. The venue
is now called the Windmill
International.

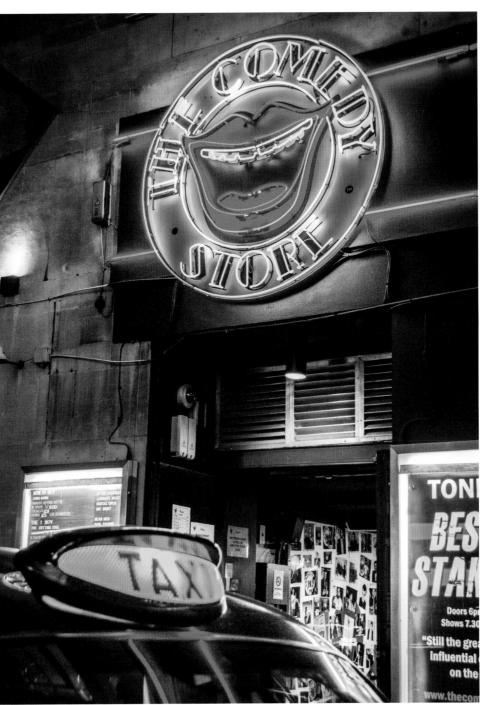

Sign at Piccadilly Circus pointing to popular attractions

Many popular London sites are just a short walk from Piccadilly Circus, including the shops on Regent Street, the cinemas of Leicester Square, Berwick Street's lively market, the restaurants of Soho, and bustling Chinatown.

Celebrating the Chinese New Year at Chinatown

Each January or February, depending on the Chinese calendar, celebrations for the Chinese New Year take place across London's Chinatown and the surrounding area, including a colourful parade, stage performances in Trafalgar Square, and a lion dance.

Lantern over Chinatown at night

Originally located at Limehouse near the docks in the city's East End, London's Chinatown has occupied its present location, between Soho and the city's theatrical district, since around the 1950s.

LEFT:

Shaftesbury Memorial Fountain, Piccadilly Circus
Built in 1819, Piccadilly Circus takes the first part of its name from the piccadil, a type of frilled collar popular in the seventeenth century, and the second from the roundabout which once stood at its centre.

OPPOSITE:

The Prince Edward Theatre on Old Compton Street
After opening as a theatre in 1930, the Prince Edward Theatre spent 40 years as first a cabaret hall and then a wide-screen cinema, until reopening as a theatre in 1978. In recent years, it has staged productions of the musicals *Mamma Mia*, *Jersey Boys*, *Miss Saigon* and *Aladdin*.

OPPOSITE:

Covent Garden at Christmas
Covent Garden is one of London's most popular festive locations. In 2018, the 115,000 Christmas lights around the market were turned on by Paloma Faith, the Kingdom Choir and members of the cast of the musical *Matilda*.

RIGHT:

Juggler performs in Covent Garden
Open every day of the year except for Christmas Day, Covent Garden is home to plenty of street entertainers: jugglers catch and balance everything from balls and batons to machete knives and chainsaws!

Harrods in Knightsbridge
In daylight, Harrods is perhaps most recognized for its trademark green awnings, which stand above its bright shop windows; at night, though, its spectacular display of lights certainly catches the eye of passers-by on Brompton Road.

Kew Gardens Pavilion
Each winter, from mid-
November to early January,
Kew Gardens opens late
for a spectacular display
of festive light and sound.
Attractions in 2018 included
300 illuminated origami boats
floating on the lake, a laser
garden, and a tunnel of lights
7m (23 ft) tall and 100m
(330 ft) long.

TOP LEFT:

Illuminated fish float through the sky at the Lumiere festival

London's free Lumiere festival of light stretches across the city each January, brightening the night with scores of illuminated art installations, from colourful fish floating through the sky to giant desk lamps and watering can lanterns.

BOTTOM LEFT:

Piccadilly at the Lumiere festival

Originating in Durham, the Lumiere festival first came to London in 2016: one notable commission that year was 195 Piccadilly by art collection Novak, which projected images from the BAFTA cinema and television archives onto the side of the BAFTA building.

RIGHT:

**The Sky Pod Bar at
20 Fenchurch Street**

The Sky Pod Bar at 20
Fenchurch Street, known
colloquially as the 'Walkie-
Talkie', offers panoramic
views of the city from 35
floors up. Its exclusive private
dining room is named after
the building's architect,
Rafael Viñoly.

OPPOSITE TOP:

**The Southbank Centre
and National Theatre**

Made up of three performance
venues – the Royal Festival
Hall, the Queen Elizabeth
Hall and the Purcell Room –
the Southbank Centre stages
more than 4000 events and
performances each year. The
Royal Festival Hall is the only
building from the 1951 Festival
of Britain still standing.

RIGHT:

Open-air screening at Trafalgar Square

In recent summers, London's Royal Opera House has put on open-air screenings of its shows in locations across Britain, including Canary Wharf, Lyric Square in Hammersmith, and Trafalgar Square. Performances in 2018 included *Don Giovanni*, *Swan Lake* and *La Bohème*.

PREVIOUS PAGES:

Skyscrapers at night

Since the turn of the millennium, the skyline of London's financial district, known as the City of London, has changed dramatically, with the arrival in 2004 of 30 St Mary Axe ('the Gherkin'), 122 Leadenhall Street ('the Cheesegrater') in 2014, and 20 Fenchurch Street ('the Walkie-Talkie') in 2015.

LEFT:

South Kensington station at night

South Kensington is home to three of London's most famous museums – the Science Museum, the Natural History Museum, and the Victoria and Albert Museum. Each hosts monthly evening events including live performances, debates and even silent discos!

Cranes and waterfront houses at Britannia Village
Built between 1994 and 2000 on the south side of the Royal Victoria Dock, Britannia Village was developed on the site of two 1970s tower blocks, Cranbrook and Dunlop Points. The cranes remain from the original dock facilities.

The sun sets behind the Houses of Parliament
Between 1899 and 1901, on visits to London and afterwards, the painter Monet produced a series of oil paintings of the Houses of Parliament, including several sunsets. Six of these paintings were exhibited at Tate Britain in 2017–18.

Transport

As London's population approaches nine million, its transport networks become increasingly important. The city's famous red buses and trademark black taxis still throng its streets, while its Underground network – the world's oldest – carries five million passengers across more than 400 km (250 miles) of track each day between its 270 stations. And London will soon welcome a new rail service, the Elizabeth Line, running from Reading and Heathrow in the west to Shenfield and Abbey Wood in the east.

As the existing transport infrastructure becomes ever busier, the city's commuters are adopting alternative routes. Cycling continues to thrive, with daily journeys by bike having more than doubled since 2000 to 670,000, thanks in part to schemes such as the TfL cycle-hire system and the London Cycle Network. And ten million passenger journeys in the past year took place on the river Thames, and there are ambitious plans to double this figure by 2035. With the Thames at the heart of the city, London's bridges remain a vital part of its infrastructure. Recent years have seen some innovative additions to their ranks, from the Millennium Bridge, whose teething problems saw it close for two years just two days after opening, to the Rolling Bridge at Paddington Basin.

Meanwhile, thousands of flights arrive in London every day at its many airports, as redevelopment work transforms them to accommodate ever-increasing numbers of flights to and from the city.

OPPOSITE:
Art deco escalators at St John's Wood station
Opened in November 1939, the Underground station at St John's Wood is now a Grade II-listed building. Its art deco escalators feature 58 original bronze uplighters and an illuminated bronze-edged roundel (right), one of only two still in existence.

Pedestrian footbridge at Canary Wharf station
This striking pedestrian footbridge leads to a new London station due to open in 2019, built on an artificial island in the West India Docks. Canary Wharf station will be part of the Elizabeth Line, and will also connect with the existing Underground station nearby.

ABOVE:
Docklands Light Railway train approaches Canary Wharf
The Docklands Light Railway opened in 1987. After several
extensions, its six branches now stretch from Stratford
International in the north to Lewisham in the south, and
from Bank and Tower Gateway in the west to Beckton and
Woolwich Arsenal in the east. Its automated, driverless trains
carry around 120-million passengers each year.

PLATFORM 9¾

LEFT:

St Pancras International station

Opened in 1868, St Pancras station was almost demolished in the 1960s, until a campaign led by poet laureate Sir John Betjeman resulted in it gaining a protected listed status. It is now the terminal for Eurostar services to mainland Europe.

ABOVE:

Platform 9¾, King's Cross

In J. K. Rowling's *Harry Potter* novels, platform 9¾ at King's Cross is where would-be wizards catch the train to Hogwarts. The actual station now hosts a recreation of that platform, where readers can have their photos taken pushing a luggage trolley through the wall.

Northern Line train leaves Leicester Square

The walls of all four platforms at Leicester Square station are adorned with designs evoking sprockets – the holes that hold film reels in place – to mark the fact that the square is home to several major cinemas.

Covent Garden station

Covent Garden is on the Piccadilly line and the station is one of the few in Central London for which platform access is only by lift or stairs. Fitness fanatics can climb the 193 steps to reach the exit.

OVERLEAF LEFT:

Inside Baker Street Underground station

Baker Street has the most platforms of any Underground station – ten – and connects five different lines: the Metropolitan, Circle, Bakerloo, Jubilee, and Hammersmith & City. The oldest platforms – like the one pictured – date back to 1863.

OVERLEAF RIGHT:

An aerial view of London Bridge Station

Open since December 1836, London Bridge is one of the world's oldest railway stations. Its 15 platforms serve more than 50 million passengers each year, making it London's – and Britain's – fourth busiest station.

ABOVE:

Diamonds and Circles at Tottenham Court Road Underground station
Recently refurbished ahead of the opening of the Elizabeth Line, Tottenham Court Road Underground station is now home to work commissioned from the French artist Daniel Buren, whose 'Diamonds and Circles' adorn the station's entrances and ticket hall.

RIGHT:

Mosaic by Eduardo Paolozzi, Tottenham Court Road station
An earlier redecoration of the station in the 1980s saw the introduction of mural mosaics by the Scottish sculptor and artist Eduardo Paolozzi; parts of these were removed during the recent refurbishment and will be reconstructed at the University of Edinburgh.

**Belsize Park
Underground station**
Opened in June 1907, the
Northern line station at
Belsize Park was – like
many Underground stations
of the period – designed by
Leslie Green, and features
his familiar oxblood red
glazed terracotta tiles and
arched windows.

Chiswick Park station
The drum-shaped ticket hall
and short square tower that
comprise the main building
at Chiswick Park station
date from 1932, when the
original station – opened in
1879 as Acton Green station
– was demolished. Chiswick
Park is on the District Line;
Piccadilly Line trains run
through the station but have
never stopped there.

OPPOSITE:

Red London buses outside Euston station

Buses were first introduced to London in 1829 by George Shillibeer, who was inspired by similar services used in Paris. The first buses went from Paddington to Bank; they carried 22 people and were pulled by a team of three horses.

RIGHT:

Heatherwick 'New Routemaster' bus drives through the snow

The 'New Routemaster' bus was introduced in London in 2012, inspired by the iconic design of the much-loved Routemaster buses that served the city from 1959 until the early years of this millennium. Some original Routemasters still run on heritage route 15H.

LEFT:

Taxis drive past Union flags on Regent Street
The first London taxis were horse-driven hackney carriages that appeared on the city's streets during the seventeenth century; licensing was introduced in 1662, and the first motorized taxis arrived in the 1900s.

OPPOSITE:

London taxis queue along Whitehall
Since 1865, it has been necessary to pass a test called 'The Knowledge' to qualify as a London taxi driver. Applicants must learn 320 standard routes through the city, covering 25,000 streets within six miles of Charing Cross.

Traffic on the Blackwall Tunnel approach
Built between 1892 and 1897, the Blackwall Tunnel originally
comprised just a single tunnel for traffic passing both ways
under the Thames. However, the volume of traffic had
increased so much by the 1930s that the decision was made
to build a second tunnel. It opened in 1967, and now carries
southbound traffic; northbound traffic passes through the
original tunnel.

203

LEFT:

Tower Bridge from inside
Built between 1886 and 1894, Tower Bridge owes its famous design to the need for river traffic to have access to the Pool of London docks. Its lower central section comprises a 'double-leaf bascule': a pair of moveable sections that can be raised to allow ships to pass underneath.

RIGHT:

Tower Bridge at night
More than 40,000 people cross Tower Bridge annually. In its first year, the bridge was raised 6000 times; today, the figure is closer to 1000, and any ship needing to pass through is required to give 24- hours' notice.

Westminster Bridge and the Houses of Parliament

The original Westminster Bridge was built between 1739 and 1750, three quarters of a century after an earlier proposal for a bridge here had been opposed by the city's watermen and the Corporation of London. The current bridge opened in 1862, designed by the engineer and architect Thomas Page with details by Charles Barry.

Rolling Bridge at Paddington Basin
The curling moveable bridge at Paddington Basin opened in 2004 and comprises eight triangular sections that can be collapsed into an octagon to allow boats to pass by. Designed by Thomas Heatherwick, it forms part of the Grand Union Canal office and retail development project.

ABOVE:

Crowds cross the Millennium Bridge on a foggy day
London's first new Thames bridge in more than a century, the Millennium Bridge was designed to carry up to 5000 pedestrians at a time. Over 90,000 people crossed the bridge on its opening day, 10 June 2000; two days later, it was closed for modifications which took two years to implement.

RIGHT:

The Millennium Bridge at nightfall
The bridge's alarming tendency to sway, which prompted its closure, was caused by a phenomenon known as 'synchronous lateral excitation': small sideways oscillations caused by pedestrians walking over the bridge are amplified by people's need to sway in time with the movement to avoid falling over. The problem was fixed by adding dampers to control the bridge's movement.

OVERLEAF:

A River Bus passes under Blackfriars Bridge
London's six River Bus services run from 22 piers between Woolwich and Putney. Aimed at commuters, they run from early morning to late evening and have on-board bars; most have space for bicycles.

Police boat patrolling the river

Established in 1798, the Marine Police Force preceded Robert Peel's Metropolitan Police Service by more than three decades. Today, the Marine Policing Unit forms part of the Metropolitan Police Service.

FAR LEFT:

Small boat sails down the Thames

Traffic on the Thames between Teddington Lock, Gunfleet Lighthouse and Margate is managed by the Port of London Authority, established in 1909 to bring order to the overcrowding and confusion found on the river in the late 1800s.

BOTTOM LEFT:

Pleasure cruiser turns on the Thames

London's pleasure cruisers offer an alternative perspective on the city's sights. Passengers can embark and alight from many of the river's 24 piers. Five new piers – at Blackfriars, Millbank, the London Eye, Tower Bridge and Westminster – were opened as part of the Thames 2000 project.

Narrowboats on the Regent's Canal
Built between 1812 and 1820, Regent's Canal helped bring
timber, coal and building materials from Northern industrial
cities to King's Cross in the heart of London. The area around
the junction where it meets the Grand Union Canal is known
as 'Little Venice'.

ABOVE:
Paddington Basin riverside
Opened in 1801, Paddington Basin formed the London
terminus of the Grand Junction Canal linking the city with
Birmingham. Since 2000, the area has been redeveloped under
the Paddington Waterside scheme, with office blocks and flats
built around the basin.

RIGHT:

Bicycle docking station at the Westfield Shopping Centre
Inspired by the Vélib' scheme in Paris, London's cycle hire scheme has seen more than 70 million journeys made since its launch in 2010. Around 13,600 bicycles can be hired from any of the city's 839 stations for £2 per day.

**Cycle Superhighway,
route CS7**
London's Cycle
Superhighways, marked by
sky blue paint, are intended
to provide cyclists on some
of the city's busiest roads
with protected spaces to
improve their safety. Route
CS7 runs from Merton in
the southwest to the City of
London, through Clapham,
Kennington, and Elephant
& Castle.

LEFT:

London City Airport

Opened in 1987, London City Airport serves 4.5 million passengers each year, flying to and from locations including Amsterdam, Edinburgh, Dublin, Zurich and Milan. Its single two-way runway is just 1500m (5000ft) long.

BELOW:

Plane lands at London City Airport

Redevelopment work at London City Airport is scheduled to finish around 2022, enabling the airport to increase its annual flights from 80,000 to 110,000. As part of this work, a digital air traffic control tower is being installed in Southampton, controlling flights from 80 miles (129 km) away.

PREVIOUS PAGES TOP LEFT:

Gatwick Airport

The UK's second-busiest airport, Gatwick handles 45 million passengers each year. It was requisitioned by the Air Ministry during the World War II and used as a base for RAF night-fighters until being decommissioned in 1946.

PREVIOUS PAGES BOTTOM LEFT:

Mosaic of the Queen at Gatwick Airport

Titled 'The People's Monarch', this mosaic was commissioned to mark the diamond jubilee of Queen Elizabeth II in 2012; the Queen reopened Gatwick in 1958 after a major renovation and returned in 1988 to open its new North Terminal.

PREVIOUS PAGES RIGHT:

Entrance to the Gatwick Express

The Gatwick Express began operations in 1984. Services run non-stop from London Victoria to Gatwick Airport every 15 minutes, taking half an hour.

RIGHT:

Aerial view of planes at Heathrow Airport's Terminal 5

Heathrow Airport's Terminal 5 opened in 2008 and is used exclusively by British Airways and its partner company Iberia. The airport's newest terminal is the entirely rebuilt Terminal 2, which reopened as 'the Queen's Terminal' in 2014.

Picture Credits